ADVENTURES

AND

EXPERIENCE

OF

JOSEPH H. JACKSON

DISCLOSING

THE DEPTHS OF MORMON VILLANY

PRACTICED IN NAUVOO

ADVENTURES

AND

EXPERIENCE

OF

JOSEPH H. JACKSON

DISCLOSING

THE DEPTHS OF MORMON VILLANY

PRACTICED IN NAUVOO

———

Originally published in 1846

ISBN: 979-8-950661-03-7
Printed in the United States of America
www.analyzingmormonism.com

CONTENTS

INTRODUCTION.

———

The following narrative of my experience in Nauvoo, is submitted to the public, that it may call attention to the character of the iniquities practiced in that city, in the name of Religion. I am aware that such is the nature of the disclosures made in the following pages — such the blackness of the record — that it will be difficult to induce men to believe that such depravity could possibly exist. From what follows, however, it will be perceived that my motives in going to Nauvoo were to gain the confidence of the Prophet, that I might discover and disclose to the world his real designs and the nature of his operations. To do this, I was obliged to practice dissimulation, and to seem to be a fit tool for him to work with. Some may say that such conduct on my part was not excusable; but let such bethink themselves that the secret designs and workings of this Heaven-daring wretch, could never have been made public only by such means as I adopted, and therefore the end justified the means. Many are the instances on record, in which bands of robbers and counterfeiters have so organized themselves as to be enabled to baffle the closest scrutiny of the law; and in such instances it has been a common practice, especially in Europe, to employ men to become seeming accomplices, that they might thus be enabled to disclose the information necessary for a conviction. This was my object; and the inducement by which I was prompted will be found in what follows.

I tell nothing more than what I have seen and heard in Nauvoo. I have colored nothing, nor set down aught in malice. Many of my statements can be corroborated by abundance of testimony. I am content, however, at present to give my story; and, if contradicted, I can follow it up by proof such as no reasonable man can doubt.

The question may be asked, how is it possible for so corrupt a man as Joe Smith is represented to be, could ever have attained a complete control as he unquestionably had over the minds of the honest portion of his followers? I confess the question puzzles me. No man, who has never seen the influence of blind fanaticism over the human mind, can imagine the effect it will produce. there were hundreds of men in Nauvoo, who, I believe, from what I have seen, had Joe Smith commanded them to commit murder in that name of the Lord, they would hare believed that they were doing God's service in obeying him. I will leave the philosophy of this for the consideration of moralists: my business is to state facts.

There is one thing peculiar that will be observed by the attentive reader, and that is, that all Joe Smith's commands, whether in public or private, were delivered "in the name of the Lord." In public, before his people, he spoke "in the name of the Lord;" and in his secret councils, if he desired the assassination of his enemy, it was "the will of the Lord" that the persecutors of the

Church of Jesus Christ should be put out of the way; and thus, in "the name of the Lord," the vilest plans for murder, fornication, and every species of crime, were carried on by this blasphemous hypocrite!

The preparation of this work was commenced previous to the late difficulties among the Mormons, which resulted in the death of the two principal witnesses to these statements, which were all made while they were alive. Yet the affidavits appended will convince the world that the assertions herein contained are based upon truth, and set forth the iniquities of the Mormons in their real hideousness. That others may not be deluded into this band of demi-devils, is an additional object for the extensive circulation of these pages.

NARRATIVE.

———

Before visiting Nauvoo, I had heard much of this famous city, and the character of its inhabitants. Such was the contrariety of reports afloat, that it seemed difficult to form any sealed opinion concerning the Prophet or his followers. When I had, however, the opinion seemed to prevail, that they were a pack of abandoned scoundrels, leagued together for the basest of purposes.

In passing down the Mississippi, in the fall of 1842, I determined to stop in Nauvoo. My object was partly to find business, and partly to gratify curiosity. With the location of the city, I was delighted; but as frequent descriptions have already gone abroad, I will not stop here to expatiate either on its beauties, or the advantages of its position.

At the time I landed, (10th of October, 1842,) there was great trouble among the saints, in consequence of a demand having been made by the Governor of Missouri, for the Prophet, for being accessory to the attempted assassination of Gov. Boggs. My visit to the city at that time, (being a stranger and out of business,) induced the people, as I afterwards learned, to believe that I was a spy from Missouri, in quest of evidence against Smith. Many men, who I have since learned belonged to the Danite Band, visited me at my boarding-house, and asked all manner of questions in relation to my business in the city. Deeming these inquiries impertinent, I did not condescend to answer them: but they did not cease their importunities. At length, being disgusted and indignant at their proceedings, I abruptly cut their acquaintance. After this, I observed that I was closely watched; but did not know the reason, until informed by a friend, that the Prophet thought me a spy. I determined then to give no satisfaction, but to pursue a silent policy.

Some time in November, I was helping to haul some goods from the river, that belonged to Messrs. Rellison and Finch. I was in company with Mr. Finch and a man from Keokuk, who was owner of the horses and wagon. We had hauled one load, and were returning for the second. As we crossed the bottom, between the Temple and the river, a man standing at about eight rods distance, (it being after dark,) called me by name. I immediately jumped from the wagon, thinking that it was a man who wished to get some goods stored that had called me. Finch immediately followed. When I got within about five feet of the villain, as he proved to be, he extended his arm at full length, and said, "Damn you, I give you what you deserve," and fired a pistol. The ball passed my head, and so stunned me, that for a few minutes I scarcely knew what I was about; but on coming to, I could scarcely see, for my face and eyes were so much burned with powder. Finch, at the time the shot was fired, was about one rod behind. He seeing me stagger, immediately pursued the fellow, but soon found that he was no match for him in speed, and gave up the pursuit. Finch and myself agreed to keep this matter a secret, that we might be able to discover some clue to the assassin. I thought that if we did not mention it, and we heard of it from others, we would be able thus to trace the matter to its fountain head. When, however, this idea became hopeless, I mentioned it to my friends, who seemed to understand the object of the maneuvre.

Shortly after this, I left Nauvoo, and went to Carthage to spend the winter. During the winter I employed my time in hunting, but I heard frequently complaints against the thieving Mormons. In the spring, I determined to find out whether Joe Smith was in reality as bad a man as he was represented, and whether he had in reality instigated the villain who attempted my life in Nauvoo.

I therefore stated to Harmon T. Wilson, deputy sheriff, that I intended to visit Nauvoo, and if any man could, I would find out Joe's plans and measures, and at a proper time, if I found him to be as base as represented, and as I believed him to be, disclose all to the world. In forming this resolution, I was actuated by a desire on the one hand to revenge myself on him, if he was guilty of the attempt on my life, and by a romantic love of adventure on the other. I possessed every advantage in person and countenance to accomplish my object, as well as a full share of experience in the ways of the world.

Accordingly, in the month of March I went to Nauvoo, and after staying there a few days, I visited Joe, and gave him to understand that I had important business with him. He invited me into his private room, and there, in the presence of Eber C.

Kimball, I disclosed the nature of my business, and made him believe that I could be of great service to him. I stated that I was a fugitive from Macon city, Georgia, and wanted *protection*. This seemed to tickle his fancy wonderfully, and throwing off restraint, he said that I was just the man he wanted, and referred me to the conduct of Joab unto David. He then said that he would make any man rich, who would be unto him as was Joab to David, and obey his commands in the name of God, that he might fulfil his prophecies. He then commenced an argument, to make me believe that he was right and lawful in the sight of God, and declared himself a godly man, and a Prophet endowed with power from on high. I then remarked, that as to his religion, I cared nothing about it, for I did not believe in the supremacy of a God. Here he looked me very steadfastly and significantly in the eye; but I flinched not. I then told him that I was a desperate man, and could release O. P. Rockwell, who was at that time confined in prison in Missouri, for his attempt on the life of Gov. Boggs. "Well," said he, "if you will release Porter, and kill old Boggs, I will give you three thousand dollars." Kimball heard this conversation throughout, but I have no hope that he could be made to acknowledge its truth, so deeply is he leagued with Joe in his villany.

Joe, after this offer, made a proposition to give me an outfit to Missouri; and said that he would soon furnish me with a splendid horse, saddle, bridle, and all the necessary accoutrements for the journey. To all of this, Kimball assented. The second morning after this, I met Joe again. He told me he had traded a town lot with Elder Grant, for a splendid black horse, and that he also had procured a saddle and bridle for the trip. "Now," said he, "go and perform in the name of God, and let the little fellow out of jail, for my heart bleeds for him." I took possession that day of the horse, saddle, and bridle; and the next day Joe brought to my boarding-house a pair of saddle-bags, concealed under his cloak. This expedition was kept a profound secret. People in general supposed that I had bought the horse of Joe, and had no idea that there was any understanding between us.

After having this horse in my possession for two or three days, Joe and I took a ride up to Edward Hunter's, where he borrowed one hundred dollars, and I drew his note for it on demand. Hunter, at this time was absent. While there, Mrs. Hunter brought the Bible to Joe, and wished him to explain some passage in the third chapter of Hosea, in relation to the adulteress. He replied that he would call at another time and translate it for her, for which she thanked him kindly. After this, I learned that the scripture named by Mrs. Hunter, was one of the proofs of the correctness of the spiritual wife doctrine, of which the reader will learn more hereafter.

After conversing a little while, we arose to depart, and Joe gave Mrs. Hunter a very sanctimonious blessing. We then got on our horses, and rode up the hill, where we were met by the Holy Patriarch Hyrum, on his white horse. He informed Joe that brother somebody, (I do not recollect the name,) was sick, and they were sent for to lay hands on him, "for he was sick unto death." I rode to the house of the invalid with them. We entered the room, and I put on a very grave countenance, while they both laid hands on the sick man, and Hyrum made a long sanctimonious prayer. As we left the house, Joe pronounced a blessing on it, and all that were within. We then again mounted our horses; Hyrum went home, and Joe and I took a ride of some five miles on the prairie. All the way out and back, he pressed me to kill Boggs; and said he would pay me well for it. Finally, I gave him a strong hint that I was in for the business; knowing as I did, if I hesitated, he would suspect me of treachery, and thus all my plans in relation to him would be frustrated. I therefore carried on my game by showing a bold front. All the while he was urging the killing of Boggs, he insisted that it was the will of God, and in God's name he offered me a reward for his blood. This was all done with an air of sanctimonious gravity, and with a look of innocence, that would make one almost believe that the Prophet really thought that he was acting under the command of Heaven. I was utterly astonished to see this man concoct the most hellish plans for murder and revenge, and yet, with pertinacity insist it was right in the sight of God! And here, (if I may be permitted to pause,) lay the whole secret of Joe Smith's success. He had a singularly unmeaning countenance, that was no index of his real character; he had so long practiced duplicity, that there was scarcely a compunctious feeling left in his bosom; and he had no scruples in regard to the means he should employ, when he had an end to attain. Hence it was, that he had no hesitancy in prostituting every thing sacred, for the purposes of lust, cupidity, or power.

The next morning after this adventure, I took my departure for Missouri. The weather was very bad, the streams high, and I suffered much with the wet and cold. After a journey of eight days, I arrived at Independence, where I put up with a Mr. Knowlton. At this time, the Chavis murderers were arrested, and I saw them in custody of the sheriff, while on their way to the jail. While these men were being put into the prison, I entered it for the purpose of seeing Rockwell, and that I might give a straight account of myself. I found him with a pair of shackles on, and a lion-skin over-coat; looked rather uncouth. There were, however, so many in prison at this time, that I had no opportunity to converse with him. My hope was, that by representing myself as being in the employ of Joe, and convincing him of that fact, to draw from him a confession that might be useful for the purposes which Harmon T. Wilson and myself had in view.

Previous to my leaving Carthage for Nauvoo, I had learned from Harmon T. Wilson, that he was in correspondence with Mr. Reynolds, sheriff of Jackson county, Missouri, in relation to another demand from the governor of Missouri, for Joe Smith. An arrangement had been entered into, that a requisition should be made on the return of Mr. Wilson, from a trip which he contemplated to take to the south, immediately on the opening of navigation. Had I thought at the time I left Mr. Wilson, of this trip

to Missouri, I should have brought a letter from him to Mr.
Reynolds, which would have disclosed to the latter my true
character. As matters, however, were, I found myself placed in a
situation where I could do no good towards the great object I had
in view. There was great excitement in Independence, in
consequence of the Chavis' murders; many persons were arriving
to join the Oregon emigrating expedition; and every stranger
appeared to be looked on with distrust and suspicion. Mr.
Reynolds was so busily engaged in arresting the Chavis'
murderers, that I could get no opportunity to make his
acquaintance, and fix upon a concerted plan of operations in
relation to Smith. Seeing the impossibility of effecting what I
desired, and having no idea of attempting what Joe sent me for, I
resolved to return to Nauvoo. Previous to taking my departure,
however, I wrote to Mr. Wilson, and directed my letter to "Point
Coupee," Louisiana; supposing that it would reach him there; but
it appears that he never received it. Having been at Independence
one week without effecting any thing, I set out on my journey. My
trip back was very pleasant; the roads having become settled, and
the weather dry. I struck the Mississippi at Churchville, crossed to
Warsaw, and thence journeyed to Nauvoo. On my arrival, I rode to
the house of the Prophet, where all seemed glad to see me; and
"sister Emma," Joe's wife, received me very cordially, the Prophet
not being at home. Since I have introduced this lady to the reader,
I will mention, that although she is acquainted with all the
villainous plans and operations of Joe, yet she should be looked on

with pity rather than scorn. I believe she knew no guile until Joe schooled her to wink at his rascality, and compelled her, by threat, to aid in carrying out his measures. Indeed, he had frequently said that it was with the greatest difficulty that he could prevail on Emma, in many cases, to hold her peace, and not expose him to the world.

In order to amuse myself until the Prophet's return, I strolled over the city, and was surprised to find so much attention paid to me; and that many, especially the women, knew all about my expedition to Missouri. This convinced me that Joe could not keep his secrets; but I did not know at that time he had so many wives to whom to disclose them. When night came on, the Prophet returned. He seemed glad to see me; and, taking me by the hand, led me into a private room, and commenced his inquiries about Porter Rockwell. He fixed his eyes steadily on me, while I gave an account of my stewardship, and suffered me to proceed about half through without interruption; when he suddenly exclaimed, "Oh! did you kill old Boggs?" "No," said I; "he was not at home;" and this was the fact, as good luck would have it, and it gave me an excellent excuse, Joe seemed to regret this very much; but soon returned to Rockwell's case, and prophesied "in the name of the Lord" that he would, after passing through the fiery ordeal of the Missouri tribulation, come safely home. He said he knew that they could prove nothing against him, for he was a true man, and they could not make him own a word of it, if he was guilty. Silence ensued for a few minutes; when Joe suddenly looked me full in the eye, and after gazing steadily for a few moments, said, "Jackson, you are the first man that I have ever met that I could not look down." Saia I, "Do you like a bold eye?" He replied that he did, and then commenced a panegyric on himself. He said that he was a good and godly man, and that he had never known wrong in his life; for, in all his acts, he was guided and protected by the power of the Holy Ghost; that the Missourians had tried to kill him, but rifle-balls could have no effect on him, for he had been shot at thirteen times in Missouri, and the balls bounded back as hail from the side of a house; and for this reason he knew the Holy Ghost was with him, and that he truly was the greatest man on the earth. To this I replied that it was altogether unnecessary for him to preach rascality to me, in the name of the Lord, for the more he did it, the less I should think of him. I then related what had occurred to me the previous fall in Nauvoo, giving him a full account of my being shot at; not letting him know, however, that I suspected him, or cared any thing about it. My object was to learn from his own lips, by seeming indifferent to the matter, whether he in reality had been black-hearted enough to send a man to perform so dastardly an act. He, however pretended perfect innocence, and could divine no reason why I had been shot at. Here ended our conversation for the evening, and Joe took me up stairs to my chamber. As he bade me good night, he pronounced the blessing of God on my head, and said that he never loved a stranger as he did me, and that he had trusted me further, for a short acquaintance, than he had ever done any man before. "But," said he, "you must kill old Boggs, and I will build you up in the world."

In order to fathom the depths of Joe's villany, I was obliged to appear to him as an abandoned wretch and outcast. When I told him I was a fugitive from justice, and had committed the darkest crimes, it seemed to give him the greatest confidence, and he immediately conceived the idea that he could through me fulfil his prophecies, and then on the top of it he would urge me to carry out his measures "in the name of the Lord."

About three days after my return from Missouri, Joe had his carriage brought out, and invited me to take a ride with him. I soon found that there was something wrong; and when we reached his Prairie farm— or, in other words, the farm of Apostle Lot, who tills it for him — I learned the secret of his depression. He took me one side, and began to talk to me about his wife: he told me he thought I had better get another boarding-house, (I was then boarding with him,) for he thought his wife loved me more than she did him. He at the same time cursed William Law, for trying to seduce his wife, which, in my opinion, was false. He continued to talk about his wife until my anger got the better of my prudence, and I then told him he must stop such conversation to me, and that I would not hear him rail out on so worthy a woman as I believed Emma to be, and threatened to knock him down if he did not cease. I told him he was a d — d rascal, and he thought every other man as black-hearted as himself. At the same time I accused him of living in fornication with other women, and that he especially should hold his peace in regard to Emma. To these aspersions he made no angry retort, but would not at that time own that he lived in fornication with other women, and said he was a godly man in every act, but that Emma was jealous of him. He then asked me if I had ever known him to do any thing wrong with the women. I replied that I had not; but that in my opinion any man base enough to concoct schemes for pillage and murder, as he had done, would lie with his mother if she would permit him. He then said it was no use to talk to me. I answered that it was not, for I had some experience in the ways of the world. We then re-entered the carriage, and rode to the city. Joe went home, and I went to Sayder's, where I had boarded previous to my trip to Missouri, and took up lodgings.

About two days after this, Joe came down the street on horseback. I met him, and told him I thought of going south, and was very sorry I could do nothing for him in Missouri, and made him believe it. He then pressed me to stay, and enter into tho manufacture of bogus; to which I consented, hoping to be able to get a clue to another branch of his villany. Shortly after this, he sent two hundred dollars to St. Louis for German plate, and went to work in a remote part of the town to fit up for operation. The details concerning the bogus operation in the city I will give in a subsequent part of this narrative.

About the time this bogus business commenced, H. T. Wilson returned from the south, and in company with him was Mr. Reynolds, the agent of Missouri, bearing a requisition from the governor of that state. When he returned, he heard reports in circulation that I had actually joined the Mormons, which so much diminished his confidence in me, that he did not come to see me, as he promised he would do. At this time, Joe was on a visit to Dixon's Ferry, and Wilson and Reynolds proceeded thither, reporting as they journeyed that they were Mormon preachers. In the mean time, word of what was on foot reached Nauvoo, directly from Springfield, from whom I do not know; but at all events, Stephen Markham and William Clayton were despatched to Dixon, to warn Joe, or to bring back word of what took place. In a few days Clayton returned, bringing news that Joe was arrested, and an order immediately issued from Hyrum for parties to start out to rescue him. One party I was placed in, and was compelled to go, to prevent suspicion on myself; it consisted of twenty-five men. Our directions were to proceed directly to Dixon, and release Joe at all hazards. I acted as pilot, and Dr. Foster proceeded ahead to reconnoiter. We were all armed with side-arms. On the prairie above La Harpe, I led the company astray purposely, that Wilson and Reynolds might get ahead. We all got lost, and wandered about for a day, without making any progress on our journey. In the mean time, another party, that had proceeded directly up the river met Joe, Wilson, and Reynolds, all in custody of the sheriff of Lee county, proceeding southwards. They escorted Joe to the city, and would not suffer the officers to take any other direction: this fact we learned, and returned to the city. At Nauvoo, the writ of *habeas* corpus, granted at Dixon, was tried before the Municipal

Court, and Joe released. Wilson and Reynolds then effected their escape from the city. Seeing all hopes of bringing Joe to justice baffled for the present, I determined to continue my game.

A few days after this, I had a private conversation with Joe, and he again wished that I should go to Missouri to serve Rockwell. I consented, and he fitted me out with a horse and sulky for my journey. My directions were to go to Liberty, and get the pistol that Rockwell shot Boggs with — it being in the hands of a widow woman of that town, with whom he had deposited it. Rockwell feared that it might be discovered and identified, and produced in evidence against him; and therefore his wife, on her return from Independence, requested Joe lo have this instrument secured.

On the morning of the fourth I started on my journey. Joe said that it was an excellent day to fool the people with, for they would think I had gone to celebrate the day at some place in the neighborhood. I crossed the river at Montrose, from thence I went to Saint Francisville, and from thence to Monticello. About five miles beyond this town, my horse became so restive from the biting of the flies, that he commenced running and kicking; the lines broke, and presently the shafts, and I saved myself by a timely leap. The horse took a circle on the prairie, and soon came back near the point from whence he started, when I caught him, and rode back to St. Francisville, where I hired a man to bring in the sulky. I returned to Nauvoo. — I neglected to mention that, when starting, Joe told me to sell the horse and sulky, and board until I could kill Gen. Donethan; but my plan was to get the pistol, and what secrets I could from the old woman at Liberty, and advise Gen. D. of what was going on relative to him. My luck, however, was bad, and my plans failed. On returning, Joe wished me to go to Missouri by water, but wanted mo to pledge myself to kill Gen. Donethan. I feigned sickness, and thus escaped further importunity.

Meantime, the bogus establishment had been moderately fitted up, and Joe suggested the idea of buying Rockwell out of prison in the fall, or just so soon as he could get sufficient manufactured to do it. Day after day passed, and I managed my card so well, that I was enabled to probe still deeper into the secret measures and transactions of this wretch. He frequently in our walks, which we took early every day, pressed me to join the church and marry; and to induce me to take a wife, he took me to houses where he kept his spiritual wives, and introduced me to them all. On leaving, he would urge me to take my choice, or at any rate to take two or three *spiritual* wives, if I did not wish to marry. I was determined, however, to form no connection with any woman, that my actions might in all things be perfectly free, and that they might hold no rod over my head.

As I have mentioned the subject of spiritual wives, I will in this place give the reader some idea of the system. The doctrine taught, is called the "spirit of Elijah," and is kept a profound secret from the people at large, and is only permitted to be known to those to whom it is given to know the "fullness of the kingdom;" in other words, the choice spirits who surround Joe, and aid in carrying his secret measures. The doctrine is found in the third chapter of Hosea; several passages from the writings of Solomon and David, and the passage, "whatsoever ye bind on earth, shall be bound in heaven." From these Scripture passages, (with which I am not sufficiently familiar to quote,) aided by revelation from Joe, as respects their meaning and construction, the doctrine is derived that there is no harm in a man having more wives than one, provided his extra wives are married to him spiritually. A spiritual wife is a woman who, by revelation, is bound up to a man, in body, parts, and passions, both for this life and for all eternity; whereas the union of a carnal wife and her husband ceases at death. When the Scripture forbids a man from taking to himself more wives than one, Joe made it refer to *carnal*, and not spiritual wives; and would frequently quote the writings of David and Solomon, to prove his position. Having an explanation of the doctrine, let us see the application. Joe had in his employ certain old women, called "Mothers in Israel," such as Mrs. Taylor, old Madam Durfee,[1] and old Madam Sessions,[2] in whom the people have great confidence; but, in fact, they are the most depraved hypocrites on earth. If Joe wished to make a spiritual wife of a certain young lady, he would send one of these women to her. The old woman would tell the young lady that she had had a vision, in which it was revealed to her that she was to be sealed up to Joe (or

---

[1] Joseph Smith was likely sealed to Elizabeth Davis Durfee in early June 1842.
[2] Joseph Smith was likely sealed to Patty Sessions between late 1842 and early 1843.

his friend, as the case may be) as a spiritual wife, to be his in time and eternity. This would astonish the young innocent; but Scripture would soon be resorted to, to prove the correctness of the doctrine, and that it was proper in the sight of the Lord. Soon after this, Joe would appear, and tell the lady that the Lord had revealed to him that Mrs. So-and-so had had a vision concerning her, and had been to see her. Not suspecting any collusion, the young lady would be astonished, and being strong in the faith, she could have no doubt but that Joe spoke by the authority of God. He would then ply his arguments, and with the utmost sanctity speak "in the name of the Lord," and say that at such a time, and at such a place, it had been revealed to him that she should be his, or his friend's, in time and eternity. If she objected, he would quote his Scripture and his revelations, and thus, by playing on her superstitious credulity, and artfully at the same time inflaming her passions, he seldom failed of his object. Being once successful, he held the fear of exposure over her as a rod to prevent rebellion from his allegiance. When, as happened in the cases of Miss Martha Brotherton and Miss Nancy Rigdon, his overtures were rejected with disdain and exposure, he threatened he would set a hundred hell-hounds on them, to destroy their reputations. This is a specimen of the mode and manner of Joe, in carrying his vile measures of seduction. To the truth of what I have here said, there are hundreds who can testify, and I have no doubt would do it, if they could be protected from the revenge of the hellish clan which still exists in Nauvoo. The extent to which this abomination was carried, may be imagined from the fact that Joe Smith boasted to me, that he in this manner, from the commencement of his career, had seduced four hundred women.

But to return to the bogus establishment. The first attempts at bogus-making were rather rough; but in October, Messrs, Barton and Eaton came on from Buffalo, having been sent by one of Joe's emissaries, and brought with them a splendid press, and all the necessary tools and materials for operation. The press was put up in the south-east room, up stairs, of the house formerly occupied by Joe, being the same room where the Holy Order had previously met. The business was then rushed ahead in good earnest, and an excellent specimen of base coin produced, Soon, the city was flooded with this money, and a report was put in circulation that bogus manufacturers were at work in the city. Joe had given out that the room occupied by the press, was rented to Messrs. Barton and Eaton, who were mechanics, and were making drafts for the machinery of a factory which they contemplated erecting. The press continued to run until they had manufactured about $350,000. The intention was to keep the press running, and purchase a large amount of stock, but being forced to remove it, by a circumstance which I shall presently relate. Joe concluded to wait until spring, when the large emigration which was expected would afford a better chance to operate. About half of the money manufactured, was put in circulation in Hancock county, and the balance sent east, or passed off to transient persons. All the twelve apostles, except Orson Pratt, and Eben C.

Kimball, were engaged in this business, and frequently visited the room where the press was, and took turns in working it. Hyrum, at the time the press was in operation, had a lame knee, and could not get out of the house; but Joe and myself frequently visited him, and discussed measures for raising the wind to purchase more stock. Joe told me, that in Ohio, he, Dr. Boynton, Lyman Wight, Oliver Cowdry, and Hyrum, were engaged with others in a bogus establishment on Licking Creek, but that their operations were cut short by the bursting of the Kirtland Bank.

While the press was suspended in its operations, a man by the name of Brown came to Nauvoo, and sold to Joe a quantity of counterfeit ten dollar Yates County bills, for twenty dollars per hundred. Joe and Hyrum have been frequently seen with their hands full of these bills, by many persons in Nauvoo, and by them the whole country was flooded. There is not a merchant in the city but knows this fact, and also that there has been a large quantity of bogus in circulation. The first who detected the counterfeit paper money, were Holdridge, Gilman & Co., of the New-York store. The large amount of spurious money afloat, caused a great excitement in the city, and it became a common talk among the most wealthy class, who were not afraid to speak their minds. The agitation of the subject very much offended His Holiness, and he, to save himself, railed out in his characteristic style, and pronounced a the curses of God on the heads of these persons, who were in fact the most substantial men in the city; such as the two Laws, Dr. Foster, F. M. Foster, C. L. Higbee, and Mr. Cole.

These men he accused of being guilty of all kinds of crime, especially of counterfeiting. This was all done to kill their influence, and in the hope that, by raising the cry of "Stop thief!" he would turn suspicion from himself.

I have stated above, that the bogus press was in operation in Joe's old house. At that time, I had laid my plans to give word to Harmon T. Wilson, and urge him to bring a *posse* down suddenly on the city and surprise the apostles at work on the the bogus press: but about this time Avery was kidnapped by a party from Missouri, aided by some citizens of Illinois, and carried into Missouri. This Avery was one of a gang of Mormon horse-thieves, that infest the whole country. Joe was exceedingly indignant at this summary mode of proceeding against one of his friends, and arrests were determined on. — Accordingly writs were got out, and one man by the name of Elliott, living in Green Plains, was taken, and brought to the city, charged with being a kidnapper. This proceeding aroused the whole country, and a report was spread in the city that the Missourians, and the people of Warsaw and Green Plains, were coming to rescue Elliott. Joe became greatly alarmed, and removed the bogus press. In consequence of this alarm, the city council was called, and raised a city police of forty horse and forty footmen, in the pay of the city, which was placed under the sole direction of Joe, and sworn to execute his orders. This police was kept in pay for several days, and disbanded, to be called out at any time occasion required.

At this time I was forced into an adventure, which was near

ending tragically. Information was obtained by Joe that a man by the name of Richardson, who lived about nine miles back of Montrose, (Iowa,) was going to Missouri, to testify against Avery, who was shortly to have his trial; he and a boy named Childs were the material witnesses to prove his guilt, and Joe determined to secure them. Accordingly, Joe selected several of his Danite Band, placing Capt. Dunham at the head, and, to try me, ordered that I should go along. I did not know at the time what was in the wind, and I consented. The company consisted of Dunham, Cahoon, Hosea Stout and brother, W. Karnes, Scoville Smoot. and myself— making seven in all.

We went to the river, and while passing over, the real object of the adventure was disclosed by the answer of Capt. Dunham to Hosea Stout, who asked what the Prophet's orders were. Dunham replied that they were to take Richardson, and bring him to him (Dunham) if they could do it alive; if not, kill him, and bury him in a dark ravine; at the same time, telling Stout to take good care and have it all done correct. He then gave Stout the command, and pronounced the blessing of God upon us all, and ordered Stout, if any man disobeyed, or attempted to back out, that they should not let him turn around more than once before they shot him; "for," said he, "dead men tell no tales." Think's I, this is a terrible scrape I have got into; I am paying too dearly for sights; for I assure the reader, that I felt horrified at the idea of such proceedings: but there was no alternative; I must go and obey, or be shot; so I put on a straight face, and determined to go it, but at all hazards, to suffer no injury to Richardson or the boy. We all mounted our horses, leaving Dunham and Cahoon to guard the boat, and rode off at a full gallop. We kept our pace until we got four miles back of Montrose, where we halted at a house, and got drink. This was about two o'clock at night. The man of the house got up and went along with us, to show the way. His name was Hunter, and he is one of the faithful. We again mounted our horses, and rode off rapidly. Little was said during the rest of the journey. When we got within about eighty rods of the house, the party stopped, and commenced talking very low. Being in the rear, I did not hear what was going on; but on riding up, they raised their voices, and Stout addressed me, saying that this Richardson was a member of their band in Missouri. What band? said I. The Danite band, replied Stout. (This was the first time I had ever heard the Danite band spoken of by the Mormons; they had generally called themselves the "High Police," in the conversations that I had had with them.) Said he, "This man is a desperate character, and he knows all of us, and therefore it will not be safe for any of us to go into the house. He don't know you, and therefore you must go in, and we will wait about ten rods off, to be on hand in case of difiiculty." I declined going alone, but he spoke fiercely, "You know my orders." I made no reply for some rods, being on a walk, when some one of the company who was near, said, "Is he going?" I replied "Yes." "Amen," they all cried. We rode near the house, and stopped. I dismounted, walked up to the door, and knocked. "Come in," cried Richardson. I entered, when his aged mother, who lay in bed on the opposite side of the room, sprung up in haste, and asked me if I was not General Rich. I replied that I was not. Then said she, "Aint you from Nauvoo?" "No," said I. She then said that these men were such a pack of liars, there was no trusting them. Said I, "What is the matter?" Again she asked if I was not from Nauvoo. "No," said I; "I never was there. I am in pursuit of a horse-thief from Burlington." By this time Richardson was partially dressed, and I asked him if I could stay all night, to which he replied in the affirmative. I then asked him if he would go with me to put up my horse. He said "yes," and drew on his boots, and got a light prepared. While this was going on, the old woman eyed me very sharply, and said that this was her son, and that he was going to Missouri in the morning, to lestify against Avery, a horse-thief; and that the reason why she suspected me to be from Nauvoo, was because they had been looking for some of Joe Smith's Danite band, to prevent him from going; and concluded by saying, "I know him of old, and he must not send his men after my son: if he does, I will have their cursed hearts out." "Yes," said I, " and I'll help you." We then left the house, to feed my horse. When we got a little distance, I told him what I wanted; he raised a shovel that was standing near the fence, and bade me not come near him. I then drew my pistol, and told him to put down the shovel, or I'd blow his brains out. Here the company came up, and I told Richardson that if he would go along, he should receive no harm. He finally consented, got his horse and mounted him, and I delivered him to the charge of Karnes. We then had another to take, the boy,

Childs, (I think that is the name,) who lived in the neighborhood. We made Richardson pilot us, but he pretended not to know exactly where the boy was, and stopped at his neighbors, as the company thought, to inquire, but in reality to give the alarm. After we got the boy, I called Stout to one side, and told him that he had foolishly let Richardson talk with his neighbors, and that there would be a plot laid to stop us. He seemed to think there was no danger, and said if it proved so, Richardson would be the first man shot. I will here say, that my plan was to release Richardson at Montrose, where I thought I could do it without being suspected by either party, by raising an alarm, and it being dark no one would know who did it. I told Stout, however, that I did not like our situation, for I did not want to be caught kidnapping, as our situation would be very unpleasant. I would have left the company immediately, had it not been that I could not benefit Richardson without exposing myself; and all I had was in Nauvoo, and I was still desired to keep up appearances with Joe, that when I did expose him, I might do it to some purpose.

When we got within a half mile of Montrose, Richardson, who had previously, by fair promises, induced Karnes to give up the halter of his horse, which he had held in his hand during most of the journey, put spurs, and ran into the town. At this time, the boy was on behind me, and of course I could make but little speed; the others, however, started after Richardson, and I expected to find them all in town. When I arrived at the old Barracks, I was surprised to find Karnes and Stout alone, sitting on their horses. I asked where the balance of the company was, but they did not know, and appeared to be waiting for them to come up. I suggested that they had gone on to town, and urged them to follow on with me. So on we went, but on arriving at Peck's store, we were surrounded by about fifteen men, whom Richardson's friends had aroused, and who were armed with guns and bayonets. They soon took off the lad from behind me, and Richardson pointed to me, and said to one of the gang, "Uncle John, this is the man that drew a pistol on me, and said he would shoot, if I did not drop my shovel." With this, the old fellow, who was very stout, seized the bridal of my horse, and ordered me to turn round, and go back to Carpenter's tavern, saying that Lynch law was good enough for me, and that I should have until sunrise to say my prayers. This made me feel rather curious, but I determined on a bold push to extricate myself. I drew my pistol, and pointing it directly at the old fellow's head, said I, "Let go my horse, or I'll blow off the cap-piece of your skull." This confounded him so completely, that he loosed his hold and jumped back. With this, I gave a loud yell, struck my horse with the pistol, and bounded through the men, who stood with fixed bayonets immediately in front of me. My horse received three bayonet-wounds, but I escaped unhurt; they fired on me, but it being too dark to see a rod ahead: they shot at random. Stout, in the meantime, escaped in the confusion, and we ran our horses to the ferry-boat, where we found the balance of the company we had lost.

We all boarded the boat, (Karnes being as we thought in possession of the people of Montrose,) and rowed for our lives over to Nauvoo. On arriving there, we found Joe partially dressed, wrapped in his mantle. He had heard the report of guns on the other side, and had got up at this early hour, which was for him very unusual, to see what had happened. On landing, we told him our story. I damned the men as a pack of cowards, for having left myself, Stout and Karnes. On learning that Karnes was still in Montrose, the Prophet raised an alarm, called out the Legion, and gave orders to pass over the river and release brother Karnes, who, he said, had been kidnapped by the Missourians. The whole city was thus thrown into confusion, and hundreds rushed to the river, and crossed over in all manner of crafts. While this was going on, Karnes was discovered in a canoe paddling across the river, above town. All hands went to meet him, and as he landed, Joe cried out "Hallelujah! Glory to God! well done brother Karnes!" &c. Karnes was utterly confounded at these demonstrations; but kept still. He could not, however, have looked meaner, had he been detected in sheep-stealing. So well did Joe managed this affair, that to this day, the people of Nauvoo generally believed that Karnes was in reality kidnapped by the Missourians; and, of course, the story was told by the people of Montrose, was set down by Joe's honest dupes to the credit of persecution. Thus ended this nefarious plot, which, had it so far succeeded as to have got Richardson to Nauvoo, the order of Joe was to tie an iron bar to his shoulders, and throw him into the Mississippi, for cat-fish food.

My action in this affair gave Joe the greatest confidence in me, and aided the belief that I was in reality a desperado. He now threw off all the restraints under which he had previously acted, and seemed no longer to doubt that I would really carry any measure of his, no matter how black or damnable. In consequence of my having made so great a conquest of his confidence by my conduct in this affair, I was admitted into all his secret councils, and was confided in so far, that he disclosed to me every act of his life, that he had occasion to refer to in conversation. By this means, I became possessed of facts in relation to the plundering, murdering, and counterfeiting operalions, in which Joe had been for years engaged, and in which he was aided by accomplices throughout the country. As these things were merely disclosed to me by Joe, I will not venture at present to mention names: but I believe that if the government and the people would raise the means, and enter in a proper spirit into measures to ferret out the villains, I could disclose facts sufficient to lead to the; detection of numbers of a band of scoundrels who infest the whole country, and have their head-quarters at Nauvoo. Yes, this far-famed Holy city of Nauvoo, has been the hiding-place of more stolen goods, horses, and thieves, than any other spot on earth; and there, under the protection of the city ordinance, which forbids an officer of justice to search for persons or property, unless the writ was first endorsed by Joe, and executed by the city marshal, they remained in perfect security.

It is not the country in the immediate vicinity of Nauvoo

that alone suffers from the depredations of these land-pirates; the whole state, and Iowa and Missouri to a great extent, feel the scourge. Yes, in Missouri, Joe Smith has his friends and emissaries. But enough of this; my object is to tell what I saw and heard of events passing before me, and not of what was transpiring at a distance. When, however, the time arrives, I will not be silent.

It was shortly after the adventure I have related above, (15th of January, 1844) that Joe informed me in conversation, that he had been endeavoring, for some two months, to get Mrs. William Law for a spiritual wife. He said that he had used every argument in his power, to convince her of the correctness of his doctrine, but could not succeed. I then asked him how he dare preach such doctrines to virtuous and well-meaning females, in the name of the Lord; and in relation to the particular course he was pursuing towards Mrs. Law. I remarked that it astonished me to see him profess so great friendship for Law, while at the same time he was endeavoring to destroy his happiness by the seduction of his wife. To this he replied that Law was trying to seduce Emma, and he was determined to beat him. I then asked him if Emma knew of his having so many spiritual wives, to which he replied that she did, and was knowing to every act of his life, and he believed she was the most virtuous woman on earth; and that she even would not be true to him if she could get a chance. "But," said he, "I watch her close, and mean to, so long as I live." I then asked him if he could blame Law if he should seduce Emma. He seemed to think that Law would not do such a thing. I then reminded him that he just said that Law *had* tried to seduce Emma, in order to justify his own proceedings with Law's wife, but now that he contradicted himself by expressing so much confidence in Law. To get out of his dilemma, he said that the truth was, Emma wanted Law for a spiritual husband, and that she urged as a reason, that as he had so many spiritual wives, she thought it but fair that she should at least have one man spiritually sealed up to her, and that she wanted Law, because he was such a "sweet little man." He then tried to persuade me to aid him in his purposes on Mrs. Law, and said that he would employ any stratagem in order to accomplish his object, and went on to say, that he and Emma had both tried to persuade her of the correctness of the doctrine, but that she would not believe it to be of God. I told him that he must carry his plot himself, for I would have nothing to do with such things; but remarked, that if all parties were agreed, that he and Law had better swop wives; to which he replied that that was all Emma wanted. The conversation then turned on other subjects, and Joe boasted of his feats and schemes, and how cunningly he had carried his measures. He spoke of his spiritual wives particularly, and called them "great captains" in his service to carry his design; and remarked that through them he could get any stranger's money. I asked him how he would work the matter; to which he replied, that he had only to tell certain of his spiritual wives, that such a man had been in the Missouri war, and that he should be put out of the way, and his property and money consecrated to the use of the church; then, said he, it is d— d easy for them to get into his good graces, and to mix a white powder with his victuals, and put him out of the way. I then told him that he ought to give me the names of these women, as they might be of great service to me in carrying his secret measures. He then went on to give me the names of women who, he said, would go to the ends of the earth for him; but I shall not in this place disclose them. My reason for silence on this point is, that the governor, to whom I disclosed all the abominations to which I refer in these pages, did not pursue the proper policy, but treated my disclosures with contempt. Had he marched to Nauvoo as was proposed, with an army, I would have been willing to pledge my life that I could have produced proof— damning proof— of every word I have said. To disclose names, when the proof was at hand, would have produced its proper effect; but to mention them in these pages would only defeat the object which I have in view. Besides this, many of Joe's spiritual wives are honest in their belief of the correctness of the doctrine, and to the world they have untarnished characters; it would not therefore be generous in me, nor would the world justify it, to disclose the names of such as are misguided and deceived, but not abandoned, and thus for ever blight their reputations. But more of this anon.

To return to Joe's attempts on Mrs. Law. For the purpose of effecting his object, he got up a revelation that Law was to be sealed up to Emma, and that Law's wife was to be his: in other words, there was to be a spiritual swop. Joe had never before suffered his passion for any woman to carry him so far as to be willing to sacrifice Emma for its gratification; but in this case, no doubt, the object was the more prized because of the difficulty of procuring it.

It may be proper here to observe, that Law, although one of the principal men of the church, yet he was not one of those to whom it was given to know "the fullness of the kingdom." Although an enthusiastic Mormon, yet he was but little acquainted with any other than matters particularly pertaining to the church. He had frequently heard of the spiritual wife doctrine from the Gentiles; but he, not having heard such doctrine taught by Smith, set it down as a slanderous persecution against the church. When, however, this new revelation was made known to him, his eyes were opened, and at once he indignantly rejected the doctrine, as not of God, but of the devil. Such was his vehemence and indignation, that it became apparent to Joe that he had presumed too much on Law's faith, and that it would be idle to attempt to stuff him with the doctrine. There was no alternative, therefore, for Joe, but to destroy Law's influence; and consequently a great bustle was raised, and Law cut off from the holy order. This placed Law, who was particularly sensitive, in an awful dilemma; and so powerfully did the frequent lectures he received work upon his nerves, that I entertained serious apprehensions that he would become crazed.

One Sunday morning; Joe and I had a long talk concerning Law, in which he avowed (not for the first time, however,) his determination to put Law out of the way; for he had become dangerous to the church of Jesus Christ, or Latter-day Saints, and that it was the will of God that he should be removed. He, however, wished to proceed in such a manner that he would be able to get Law's wife. He then determined on calling out the police, as it was publicly termed, (but Danites. in private,) of which the city council had given him the sole command, with power to disband or hold them on duly at his discretion. He determined to keep forty of them on duty, twenty at a time, under pay of the city. The reason for this proceeding, as given to the people, was, that he thought it necessary to have a city watch; but the real object, as disclosed to me, was to murder his enemies. These men were, as Joe told me, sworn to the following oath:

> "You do, each and every one of you, having the power
> of the Holy Ghost conferred upon you by the first
> Presidency of this Church, swear that you will protect
> me and my household in every measure that I may
> deem lawful in the sight of God or that I consider
> necessary to the prosperity of the church of Jesus
> Christ of Latter-day Saints — MURDER and
> TREASON not excepted — so help you God."

After having given me the substance of the oath, he remarked, that he could through these men do the thing up nicely. Not only was his design to remove William Law, but also William Marks. The spite he had against the latter, arose from the fact, that he had endeavored to seduce the daughter of Marks, and she had informed her parents, who were very wrathy, and Joe dreaded their influence. For this reason, he said that these individuals, if they were not checked, would ruin the church. Now, said he, I will work in this way: — I will keep twenty on watch, under the command of Capt. Dunham, who will select five to do the work, and these men will both be missing, and then I'll make a great noise about it, and call it persecution." "Now," said he, "aint this a d — d I good plan to get rid of traitors? But," continued he, "you must keep this from Emma, for she thinks so much of Law, that she won't submit to it." I replied that I would. He then said that he intended to keep up this watch until he had rid the city of his enemies, and there were some in the country whom he also intended should go by the board. He said that the church had already suffered enough from persecutors, and that he would submit no longer: men must cease their persecutions, or he would give them a dose that would stop them. I had listened patiently, thus far, to the mad and hellish schemes of this wretch, when I took a bold and decided stand in opposition to him. I took the part of Law and Marks particularly, for they were the only ones in immediate danger. Joe accused me of tying his hands, and said that he could do nothing if opposed. In the meantime, a Mr. Norton, who had become by some means possessed of the facts, gave Law a hint of what was going on. Emma had also overheard something to arouse her suspicions, and I kept the matter in limbo by hammering at Joe in private. Soon, the plot became almost visible. The people grumbled greatly at the immense expense of the forty guards which were kept in pay, without any good cause being assigned, and suspicion was aroused throughout the city, that some underhand work was in contemplation. Wm. and Wilson Law having heard, by the vague information they had received, that either one of them or Marks was the Judas whom Joe sought, armed themselves, and went to Joe's house. On seeing them, Joe became desperately alarmed, and gave every evidence of his apprehension. They had a long conversation, in the course of which Joe made some abusive remark, which so exasperated Wilson Law, that he drew his pistol, and made Joe swallow his words in a hurry. So great was the excitement, that it was with difficulty that William Law and Hyrum Smith, could prevent Wilson from firing.

Joe, seeing his plans foiled, determined on making capital of the whole affair, by raising the cry of persecution. Accordingly he called the city council together; and in order to show the public that there was no ground for the rumors that had been afloat concerning the plot against Law, he brought all the forty guards up, and questioned every man whether he had bound them by a severe oath. Every man appeared perfectly amazed, and not one had ever known of any such thing, nor did they know any thing about the conspiracy against Law and Marks. This is a part of Joe's game: whenever he is accused of secret plots, he calls his men, who are instructed to appear as foolish as possible to disprove the accusation. In this instance, they endeavored so hard to appear silly, that a sensible man might have defected the trick; but the faithful were convinced that Joe had been vilely persecuted and slandered, and that there was no ground whatever for the accusation against him. Joe, after having proved himself innocent by his accomplices, turned on the old man Norton; and, calling him all manner of vile names, told him his tongue ought to be pulled out by the roots; and said he, "D — n you, if you I ever give vent to such another rumor, without more cause, I will order you cut up and fed to the cat-fish." This was in presence of the city council, and a large number of spectators. The poor old fellow, who was a true Mormon and an honest man, really thought that the indignation of Heaven was let loose upon him, and he looked the very image of penitence and submission. After delivering himself of his rage on the old man, Joe turned to the city council, and declared that he was Law's warmest friend; and so completely did he spread the deceit on them, that the Laws were induced to keep what had passed between them and Joe to themselves, and to the world every thing appeared fair. Law did not know that I had any knowledge of what passed, until I gave him a hint of his danger, and then disclosed what I knew of the affair that had transpired between him and Joe. From that day we had a perfect understanding.

To prevent an interruption of my narrative, I have omitted an interview that I had with Joe and Hyrum, at the time the plan to assassinate Law was first concocted.

Previous to Joe having settled upon any particular plan for

the removal of Law, he sent for Hyrum to counsel with him. We all three took a walk down the river bank, and Joe made known to Hyrum that he had told me the whole plot against Law's life, which appeared to please him; but he opposed Joe's plan of assassination, and stated that if Law was cut off in this manner, it would bring the whole Gentile world down on them. He then suggested what he called a better plan of operation, which was to win Law's friendship by appearing sorry, and apologising for what had happened and then invite him to a party, where they could easily put a white powder in his tea. Joe thought a few moments on the plan, and said that Emma would be in the way, and she would not suffer it. Hyrum met this objection by saying, that he would get his wife to call off Emma's attention, and then Mrs. Thompson and Mrs. Durfee would do up the business; Law would be taken suddenly ill, they would be called to lay hands on him, and no one would suspect the cause of his death. This course he deemed much safer than Joe's; because by his plan there would be suspicion and trouble. Joe said he would take the evening to think of it; soon after, we arrived at the Nauvoo House, and Joe went home, Hyrum and myself then proceeded alone to Joe's store. I proposed to walk back of the store to the river; being desirous to get something further out of him. I then asked him some questions about Mrs. Thompson, whether she could be trusted, &c. I told him that I did not want her acquaintance unless she was one of the secret women. He replied that I need have no fears of her, for he would trust her with his life. Said be, "If I were to tell her to put on men's clothes, and set Law's mill on fire, she would do it. "Oh! my God! she is a captain." I then remarked that I had heard that she was one of his spiritual wives, and now I did not doubt it. Said he, "Who told you?" I replied the Prophet told me, not only of her, but of nearly all their secret women, and it was right that he did, for they might be of service to me in carrying their measures. "Yes!" said he: "I have slept between her and my wife." "My God," said I, "how did you keep them from quarreling?" "Oh!" said he, "they are sisters; and that is not all, they are one in Christ Jesus." He then went on to give me a history of his feats with his spiritual wives, but, for reasons above mentioned, I will withhold names.[3]

There are women, however, who should be exposed, such as this Mrs. Durfee. Taking her own confession and Joe's stories as correct, there is not, I believe, such another perfect fiend in human shape on the earth. A more devout, pious and virtuous being, than she apparently is, cannot be found in any church; but a more perfect specimen of knavery, villany and every thing that is detestable in humanity, than she in reality is, the Union cannot produce. A stranger who visits Nauvoo can form no idea of the corruption practised in the city. To him every thing appears perfectly quiet and harmonious, and he is favorably impressed; and hence, sets down all he hears against the Mormons, as

-----

[3] In 1869, Mercy R. Thompson signed an affidavit that he was married or sealed to Hyrum Smith by Joseph Smith in the presence of her sister. They were married or sealed in 1843. Mercy's first husband passed away in 1841. (see Joseph F. Smith Collection, Affidavit Book 1:34, LDS archives; typed copy)

originating in religious intolerance. Nay, a man may live for years in this place, and know but little of its iniquities, so completely does Joe cover up his crime. Many who were disposed to tell what they knew, were deterred, and are still deterred by the fear of the power of Joe and the secret clan about him. When any thing of a disgraceful character is disclosed, Joe, ever ready to prove a negative, will bring together his clan, and prove himself perfectly innocent; and thus, no matter how vile his conduct in private, the individual who ventures to disclose it, not only runs the risk of his life, but has but little hope of making the people believe his story. Joe's conduct with the women of Nauvoo, surpasses every thing in blackness, that I have ever heard or read of. I have from his own mouth, and from the mouth of his victims, statements which I dare not reveal; for the world will not believe that such corruption could possibly exist. Yet, if protection could be afforded to some of those females who were the victims of these wretches (the leaders in Nauvoo,) I could I believe from their own mouths, procure confessions that would startle the world. I have visited frequently, those women whom Joe supported for the gratification of his lust; I have found them subsisting on the coarsest food, and not daring to utter a word of complaint, for they feared Joe Smith more than they did their God. I have appealed to the finer feelings of their nature, and seen them weep as children, when dwelling on the degraded state to which their credulity had reduced them. Knowing me to be in the confidence of Joe, they hesitated not to unfold their griefs to me, but their neighbors and acquaintances generally know nothing of their feelings or their degradation. These remarks apply only to a portion of the spiritual wives, for there are many who are as corrupt as Joe himself.

From my knowledge of the spiritual wife system, I should think that the number of secret women in Nauvoo cannot be much less than six hundred.[4] There are many married, as well as single women, in this number; and so slyly do they carry on their operations, that the husbands of many have never mistrusted the fact. Occasionally, a matter of this kind was detected, that opened the eyes of a few persons; and so conspicuous were things made to appear the early part of this spring, that every man in the city, who was not so blinded by fanaticism as to doubt the evidence of his own senses, could have seen what damnable iniquity was practiced. In consequence of the discoveries then made by the two Laws, Dr. Foster and others, and the exposure that followed, many of the most intelligent and respectable of the church dissented, denounced Joe as a fallen prophet, and formed a new society.

But to return to my conversation with Hyrum. After giving me his experience in the spiritual wife system, he urged me to take a few women, and named two or three whom he said would suit me. I thanked him, and said I had no desire to form any connection with any women in the city, but if I should change my mind I would give his choice the preference, in part. As we

---

[4] While this number is exaggerated, others like Sarah Pratt also claimed high numbers saying that Joseph had "many more" wives than eighty [Wilhelm Wyl, *Mormon Portraits* (1886; repr., Springfield, MO: Analyzing Mormonism, 2026), 62].

returned to the store, we met Dr. Richards, and Hyrum said to him that he would prophecy on my head that I would soon come into the church, and become as great a man as ever Paul was. To this I made but little reply, and left them together. I went down to Joe's house, and on entering, I found Joe in conversation with Emma, who was weeping bitterly. I asked Joe if he was engaged. He replied by telling me to walk into his council-room, and he would be there presently. I accordingly went in, and found Porter Rockwell sweeping the room. After I took my seat, Rockwell remarked that there was trouble in the camp. Said I, "Yes, and it appears to be of a serious nature." Presently Joe entered, and took his seat beside me. He appeared vexed with Emma, because she opposed him in his plans against Law. He said she was mad because she could not get Law for a spiritual husband, and that he should be obliged to turn off the spiritual wives that he kept about the house.

Accordingly, in a few days Joe broke up house-keeping, and Ebenezer Robinson took the house. Joe and all his family boarded with him; and thus ten or twelve poor females whom he had duped, and some of whom who really thought that they had the Holy Ghost for a bed-fellow, were turned out of house and home to shift for themselves. Joe's reason, as given to the people, for thus breaking up house-keeping, was that he had too much business, and had not time sufficient to attend to both household concerns and the affairs of the church.

But to return to my conversation with Joe in the

council-room He said that he had come to a firm determination that no traitor should live in the city, and that there were some in the country who he said should go by the board. He named Laws, Doctor and C. A. Foster, Higbee, Kilbourn of Fort Madison, Fleak of Keokuk, Sharp, Col. Williams, H. T. Wilson and A. Simpson, who, he said, were a pack of persecuting d — d rascals, and were continually sapping his heart's blood by their influence; and, continued he, "I will prophecy in the name of God that every one of the d — d vipers shall be cut off.— There," said he, "I have said it in the name of Almighty God, and one by one they shall be missing, and my prophecy fulfilled to the letter. Now don't you oppose me, for you will weaken my arm." I scarcely knew which to be the most astonished at, the infernal villany, or the mad presumption of the wretch. He seemed to think that he could, with perfect impunity, rid the country of his enemies. I have no doubt that he could, so far as law is concerned; but past experience should have taught him to fear the vengeance of an excited multitude. After giving me this caution, he remarked that if would strengthen his arm, he would build me up in the world. It was shortly after this conversation, that I commenced my opposition to him, concerning his plot against Law; this I did not do, however, until I saw his plan of operation was matured. When this was made apparent, I took a bold stand, and in the presence of his secret council, and of several of his Danites, I denounced the plot, as a foul, cowardly and damnable piece of villany. He soon saw that I was not what he had imagined me to be, and as a stepping stone to the accomplishment of his great object, he laid a plot for my removal. He appeared, if any thing, more friendly than ever, and I began to mistrust treachery; but for some time could get no evidence, until at last some of his women disclosed that a plot was on foot against me.

In the mean time, I endeavored to talk him out of his plot against Law, and gave Law a few hints of his danger, but not of a pointed or definite character, for fear that he would be hasty, yet sufficient to put him on his guard. In order that I might be able to get all the information I desired, concerning the secret designs against me, I commenced a correspondence with Hyrum Smith's daughter, and so completely won her confidence, that she watched every movement, and reported to me her observations. From her, I obtained many valuable items, and amongst the rest, the truth of a certain rumor that had been afloat in town, concerning Joe's having feigned a revelation, that he should have the wife of William Smith married to him spiritually. This was in the winter of 1842-'3, while William was in the Legislature, and previous to my last residence in Nauvoo. His wife wrote to him, and told what overtures Joe had made, which greatly exasperated William, and produced quite a disturbance in the Holy City. When William returned to Nauvoo, he gave the people's Prophet a grand flogging. Lavina, (Hyrum's daughter) in her conversation with me, declared the above statement true, and said that was not the worst. I pressed her to tell me all, and finally she said that about the latter part of May, 1843, Joe had feigned a revelation to have Mrs.

Milligan, his own sister, married to him spiritually. This was just after William Smith had left Nauvoo to preside over a branch of the church at Philadelphia; Joe and he having hushed up their differences. When this revelation was made known to Mrs. Milligan, she wrote to William, giving an account of Joe's conduct, and said that she should go back to the state of Maine, and spend the summer. When she received an answer from William, she accordingly did go. In his answer, William gave Mrs. Milligan a good piece of advice concerning Lavina; and cautioned her not to let Joe get the advantage of her. Previous, however, to this answer arriving, Joe had a revelation concerning Lavina, who was at that time living with him, and attending on her grandmother. Lavina went to her aunt, Mrs. Milligan, for advice, and inquired of her if this was lawful in the sight of God. Mrs. Milligan told her not to submit, and wept bitterly to think Joe was so base as first to try to seduce William's wife, then his own sister, and lastly his niece. She advised Lavina to leave Joe's house, and to shun it as she would a house of ill fame. Accordingly, Lavina did so.

About this time, I had a conversation with Joe, (who, it will be recollected, still professed great friendship for me, doubtlessly for sinister purposes,) which turned on the spiritual wife doctrine. Joe had been drinking quite freely, and I broached the subject of the rumor concerning Mrs. Milligan and Lavina. Joe would not own that he had tried his own sister, but confessed the whole matter in relation to Lavina, and said that he got Hyrum to consent to it, by giving him one of his spiritual girls, whom

Hyrum loved dearly, (a Miss S.[5]) He said that he had lost Lavina by the foolishness of Clayton; but, said he, "I'll have her yet." This William Clayton is one of Joe's private clerks, and a ready cat's-paw for all manner of base work. He has lived with his wife and wife's sister in common for the last year, and has children by both of them.[6] This is the man Joe had set to work to lead his niece into the paths of iniquity, aiding him by feigned revelations. But this innocent girl had timely warning from her aunt, who admonished her not to hearken to the foul councils of her father and uncle, and was thus saved from the pit into which so many had fallen. In relation to Mrs. Milligan, I would observe, that although not personally acquainted with her, I have frequently heard her spoken of by Joe's spiritual wives, who never failed to eulogize her as a noble and excellent woman. I have heard some of them say, after my depicting their desperate condition to them, "Oh that I had taken the advice of Mrs. Milligan! I might then have been saved from all this infamy to which I am now reduced." From which it will appear that Lavina was not the first she had warned.

As before stated, when Joe saw that I was in opposition to his dastardly and black-hearted measures concerning Law, he began to plot against my life; but having several confidants

---

[5] On January 27, 1846, Louisa Sanger was sealed by proxy to Hyrum for eternity [Gary James Bergera, "Identifying the Earliest Mormon Polygamists, 1841–1844," *Dialogue: A Journal of Mormon Thought* 38, no. 3 (2005): 28].
[6] William Clayton and his first polygamous wife, Margaret Moon, had a son named Daniel Albert Clayton, born Feb. 18, 1844 [Bergera, "Identifying the Earliest Mormon Polygamists," 50].

amongst the women, I kept the windward of him, but determined, to leave the city as soon as I could settle some business that I had on hand. The first plot that I learned of, was to get up a California expedition, and murder me on the route. I had lived in California, and Joe knew that I had crossed the prairies. He therefore proposed to send under my direction a company of his Danites to California, to explore the country, and look out a situation for a branch of the church. This thing was talked of for several days, without my suspecting the object. A certain lady, however, who had heard Joe, Hyrum and Dr. Richards in conversation, came to me, and gave me to understand what was going on; and told me that the plot was to get started, and kill me; and then return, and report that the Indians had shot their pilot, and they were obliged to return. This she declared was the sole object of the California expedition, and she made me swear that I would never divulge her name. She is a young lady, and lives yet in Nauvoo, and she is obliged to live there, and I would be very sorry to give her any trouble while she is yet in bondage. I had good reason to believe this lady's statements, for they came from the purest motives, and as soon as I refused to go to California, the whole matter dropped, and I heard no more of the expedition.

The next plot which I heard of, was, for Willard Richards to invite me to go with him hunting on the Island. There several men were to be placed in ambush, who would shoot me, and run towards the city, and cry "Mob! persecution! Missourians!" This plot was also revealed to me by a young lady, who wished much to

serve me. Shortly after this revelation, Richards met me in the
street, and proposed a hunting excursion on the island. I made an
evasive reply, and gave him a significant hint as to his object.

Another plot, which was detected in the execution, was
this: I slept, at Snyder's, on the ground floor, immediately under a
window. One night I was awakened by a kind of nibbling noise like
that of the gnawing of a rat. A curtain was drawn across the
window, and the assassin was attempting to cut the putty from
the glass, and then draw the curtain aside that he might make a
sure shot. On hearing the noise, I arose gently in bed, and seized
my pistol. The villain, however, heard the noise, and fled. The next
morning the tracks of his feet were visible, the cutting of the putty
from the glass was also witnessed, and in the haste of the retreat,
the fence had been knocked down. These things were seen by
many of Snyder's family, and others, who will substantiate my
statement. After the last evidences being presented to me of Joe's
intentions on my life, I went several times to see him, but could
never find him. He was sick or absent, or some such excuse was all
the satisfaction I could get. O. P. Rockwell had the impudence
once to ask me "what my business with the General was." I replied
that that was a matter between him and me. My determination
was to beard him in his villany, and, if he gave the slightest
provocation, to shoot him. Shortly after the last-mentioned
attempt on my life I left the Holy City.

As regards Lavina Smith, I should not have mentioned her
name, if it were not that William Smith last spring, in St. Louis,

gave me the same statement in regard to Joe's treatment of her, Mrs. Milligan and of his wife, which I have detailed above. William remarked, that Mrs. Milligan had always thwarted Joe, and she always would; and the reason why Joe had treated him as he had, was because he had always opposed him in his diabolical schemes of assassination. I believe that William is too honorable a man, to deny this statement: indeed, at one time, it would have taken but little provocation to have induced him to have exposed Joe and all his schemes of villany.

I have now given a brief sketch of some of the damnable practices carried on, in the name of religion, in Nauvoo; but, to avoid an interruption, I have omitted to narrate several matters that occurred before my observation. The world is generally aware of the fact, that Joe Smith was a candidate for the Presidency. This excited universal contempt and merriment; for no one considered that Joe had any idea of his own success; but he had his friends even in this, which was more treasonable and deeper; laid, than a person unacquainted with him could imagine. His object was simply this: — There was a Mr. Brown, formerly of Rushville, Ill., with whom I became acquainted in Nauvoo, soon after my arrival there. This man has a wonderful genius for invention, and has planned a submarine battery and a steam fire-ship, which, to all appearance, is capable of great execution. He stated to me, that he had been operating for twenty-one years, in perfecting this work, but had not the means to bring the matter before the nation, and that Joe had made him a proposition, which had caused him to remove to Nauvoo. This proposition was, to furnish the means to take him, together with G. A. Adams and Orson Hyde, to Russia, where the invention would be laid before the Emperor; and as Joe had great faith in its success, he expected a large sum for the secret, which Brown and Joe were to divide. This was palmed off on Brown, but was far from being Joe's real object. His real object, as he disclosed it to me, was this. He would first run for President, and thus be able to prove to the Emperor of Russia his strength in the Union. He would then send G. A. Adams, Orson Hyde and Brown to Russia, and after the utility of the invention had been fairly proved to the Emperor, Joe's proposition to him was to be submitted; which was to form a league for the overthrow of the powers that be. Now this may seem too ridiculous for any man to believe possible; nevertheless, no one acquainted with the excessive vanity of Joe Smith, will doubt but that he in reality believed that he could form even so preposterous a union. Joe's idea was, that by the aid of Brown's invention, he could introduce himself to the Emperor, and having the strongest faith in the efficiency of the new discovery as an instrument of warfare, he imagined, that if his Majesty could once see the wonderful work, that he would be willing even to take him as a partner in the benefits, for the sake of its advantages. As wild as this scheme may seem, it is no wilder than many that have characterized Mormonism from its infancy.

I deem it proper here to mention, that I told Gov. Ford, after his arrival at Carthage, of the substance of what I have disclosed in these pages; and moreover, that I would pledge myself, if a *posse* sufficient for protection were furnished, that I would go to Nauvoo, and show the secret passages and hiding places in the city, and furnish evidence of the strongest character to substantiate the truth which I had stated to him in relation to the bogus operations, spiritual wife iniquity, plans of assassination, tampering with the police, &c. An order was given at one time, to march the forces to Nauvoo, as I supposed for that purpose, but after the arrival of a certain politician, things took a turn; the order was countermanded, and the troops were disbanded on the prairie while on their march. The world is aware of what resulted from their separation in consequence thereof. The limits of these pages exclude any further remarks on this subject.

APPENDIX.

———

THE following affidavits, from men of unquestionable veracity, are appended as corroborative evidence of the truth of the statements in the preceding pages, and require no comment. They speak for themselves.

State of Illinois,
Hancock County,

BEFORE the undersigned, a Justice of Hancock, state of Illinois, personally appeared Harmon T. Wilson, who being sworn deposeth and says: That in the latter part of the winter, and early in the spring of 1842, he had several conversations with Joseph H. Jackson in relation to the taking of Joe Smith on a writ which was expected from Missouri. Jackson then proposed, that he would go to Nauvoo, and gain, if possible, the confidence of Smith, that he might be able to ferret out of his villany, and co-operate with the agent of Missouri and myself in arresting Joe, and bringing him to justice, to which proposition I assented. And further this deponent saith not.

H. T. WILSON.

Sworn and subscribed before me, this fourteenth day
of August, A. D. 1844.

GEO. ROCKWELL. J. P. [L. S.]

———

State of Illinois,
Hancock County,

PERSONALLY appeared before me, an acting Justice
of the Peace, in and for the county of Hancock,
Michael Barnes, first being duly sworn, deposeth and
saith, that some time during the winter or spring of
1843, Joseph H. Jackson was going to the city of
Nauvoo, to ferret out the iniquity of Joe Smith; that he
(Jackson) believed Joe Smith had him (Jackson) shot at
during the winter, and that he (Jackson) determined
to have revenge. And further this deponent saith not.

MICHEL BARNES, JR.

Sworn to and subscribed before me, this 13th day of
August, A. D. 1844.

R. F. SMITH, J. P. [L. S.]

———

State of Illinois,
Hancock County,

Benj. A. Gallop, after being duly sworn, deposeth
and saith: That whilst on business at Nauvoo on the
24th or 25th of June, A. D. 1843, in conversation with J.
H. Jackson, I came to the conclusion that he (Jackson)
was a spy on the character and conduct of Joe Smith,
the Mormon Prophet, for purposes unknown to
deponent. And further this deponent saith not.

BENJ. A. GALLOP.

Sworn to and subscribed before me, this 13th day of
August, A. D. 1844.

ROBT. F. SMITH, J. P. [L. S.]

———

Thomas L. Barnes, after being duly sworn, deposeth
and saith: Some time in December, 1842, I was in
Nauvoo on business; while there I fell in company
with Mr. Joseph H. Jackson. He informed me that a
few evenings previous to that time, he had been shot
at by some person unknown to him, and believed it to
be some of Joe Smith's followers. I then asked him
(Jackson) to come with me, and spend the remainder
of the night at my house. Whilst there I frequently

heard Jackson speak of Joe Smith's followers; he said
he believed Joe Smith as grand a villain as ever lived,
and that he believed he could get into his confidence,
and thereby expose his iniquities, which he said he
was determined to do.

   John Finch, Esq., informed me that he was present
and in company with Jackson when he (Jackson) was
shot at; and picks the powder out of his face, that was
blown in by the discharge of the pistol. And further
this deponent saith not.

THOMAS L. BARNES.

Sworn to and subscribed before me, this 13th day of
August, A. D. 1844.

R. F. SMITH, J. P. [L. S.]

State of Illinois,
Hancock County,

   PERSONALLY appeared before me, an acting Justice
of the Peace, in and for the country aforesaid,
Alexander Barnes, and after being first duly sworn,
deposeth and saith, that at different times in the
course of the winter and spring of 1843, Joseph II.
Jackson did state to me that he intended to go to

Nauvoo, for the purpose of ferreting out the iniquities that were practiced by Joe Smith and his gang, and that be (J. H. Jackson) believed that Joe Smith caused the attempt to be made upon his life by shooting him, upon a certain occasion at night, in the early part of that winter, and that he (Jackson) was determined to have revenge. And further this deponent saith not.

ALEXANDER W. BARNES.

Sworn to and subscribed before me, an acting Justice of the Peace, in and for said country, this 13th day of August, A. D. 1844.

R. F. SMITH, J. P. [L. S.]

— THE END —